SATURN

BY LAURA HAMILTON WAXMAN

LERNER PUBLICATIONS COMPANY • MINNEAPOLIS

Lerner Publications Company
A division of Lerner Publishing Group, Inc.
241 First Avenue North
Minneapolis, MN 55401 U.S.A.

Website address: www.lernerbooks.com

Library of Congress Cataloging-in-Publication Data

Waxman, Laura Hamilton.
    Saturn / by Laura Hamilton Waxman.
      p.   cm. — (Early bird astronomy)
    Includes index.
    ISBN 978-0-7613-4154-3 (lib. bdg. : alk. paper)
    1. Saturn (Planet)—Juvenile literature. I. Title.
QB671.W39 2010
523.46—dc22   2008027086

Manufactured in the United States of America
2 – BP – 7/1/10

CONTENTS

BE A WORD DETECTIVE

Can you find these words as you read about the planet Saturn? Be a detective and try to figure out what they mean. You can turn to the glossary on page 46 for help.

astronomer	elliptical	spacecraft
atmosphere	orbit	telescope
axis	rotate	year
day	solar system	

Can you see the planet
Saturn when you look up
at the dark night sky?

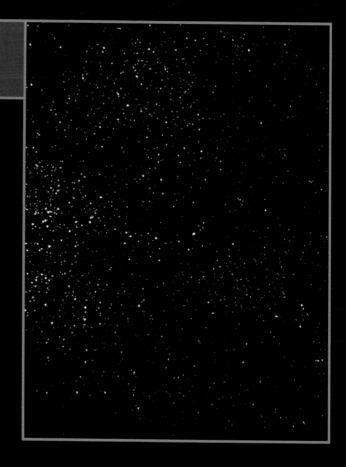

CHAPTER 1
SATURN IN THE SKY

Night has fallen. The sky is clear and black. You can see thousands of stars twinkling in all that darkness. Some planets are shining too. One of them is Saturn.

6

Saturn is the farthest planet we can see with our eyes. People have known about Saturn for thousands of years.

Long ago, the ancient Romans lived in Italy. They believed in many gods. The ancient Romans named the planet Saturn after their powerful god of farming.

This statue of the Roman god Saturn is in a museum in Rome. The ancient Romans named the planet Saturn after this god.

Saturn looks like a golden star in our night sky. But stars make their own light. Planets reflect light from the Sun.

Sometimes Saturn is hard to see. It is easier to see the planet with a telescope (TEH-luh-skohp). A telescope makes faraway objects look bigger and closer.

Telescopes give us a better look at objects in outer space.

Saturn can be seen much better with a powerful telescope. Six of its moons look like dots in this photo.

A telescope shows something special about Saturn. Saturn has wide rings. These rings circle the planet. Together, the rings look like a flat doughnut.

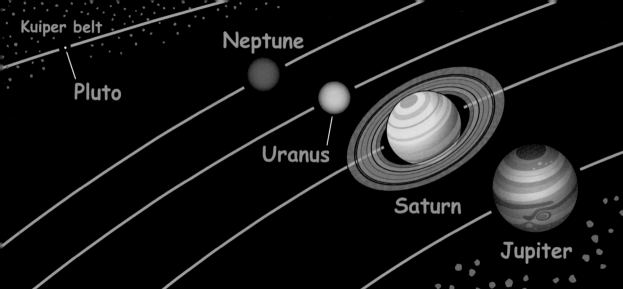

Kuiper belt

Neptune

Pluto

Uranus

Saturn

Jupiter

CHAPTER 2
SATURN'S NEIGHBORHOOD

Saturn and Earth are both part of the solar system. The solar system includes the Sun and eight planets. Smaller rocky objects called asteroids (A-ster-oyd) and comets are also part of the solar system. So are dwarf planets. Dwarf planets are larger than asteroids and comets. But they are smaller than the main planets.

This diagram shows planets and objects in our solar system. The asteroid belt and Kuiper belt are groups of rocky and icy objects.

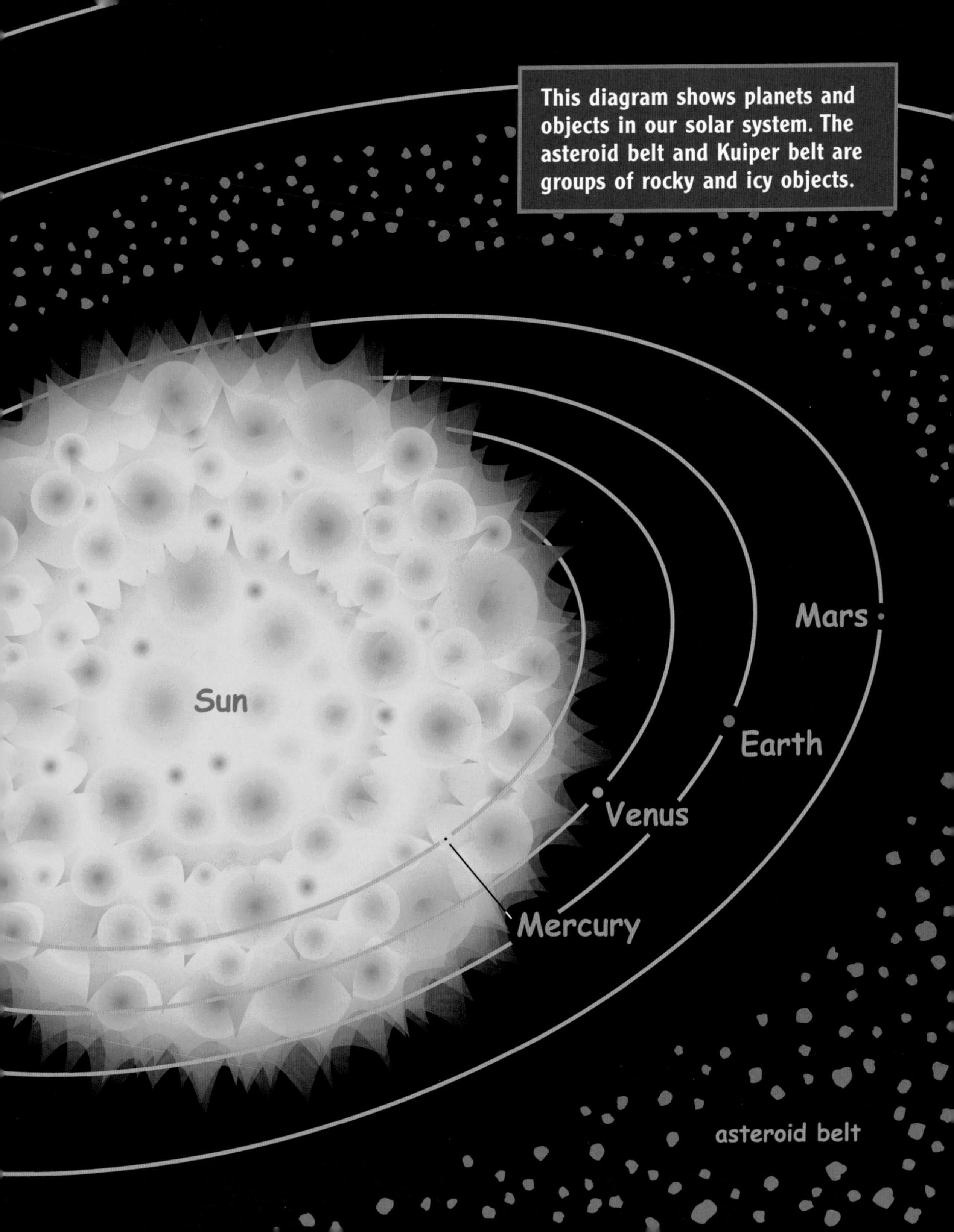

Mars

Earth

Venus

Sun

Mercury

asteroid belt

The Sun lies at the center of the solar system. The planets closest to the Sun are Mercury, Venus, Earth, and Mars. They are mostly made of solid rock. Scientists call them the rocky planets. Jupiter, Saturn, Uranus, and Neptune are mostly made of gas. They are called gas giants.

Mercury Venus Earth Mars Jupiter Saturn Uranus Neptune Pluto

This picture shows the eight planets in our solar system. The Sun appears on the left, and the dwarf planet Pluto is on the right. This picture shows all eight planets in order.

Saturn is huge!

Saturn is the second-largest planet in the solar system. Only Jupiter is bigger. Saturn is about 75,000 miles (120,000 kilometers) wide. It is as wide as nine Earths placed side by side.

A car ride from Monument Valley to Moab, Utah, might take about 2½ hours. A spacecraft traveling at the same speed would take more than 1,600 years to fly from Earth to Saturn.

Saturn is the sixth planet from the Sun. About 886 million miles (1,427 million km) stretch between the Sun and Saturn. Imagine a highway that long. Now imagine a car going 60 miles (97 km) an hour. That car would take more than 1,600 years to drive from one end of the highway to the other.

The planets in the solar system are always moving. Each planet follows its own path around the Sun. The path is called an orbit. The planets' orbits are oval shaped. Scientists call this shape elliptical (ih-LIHP-tih-cuhl).

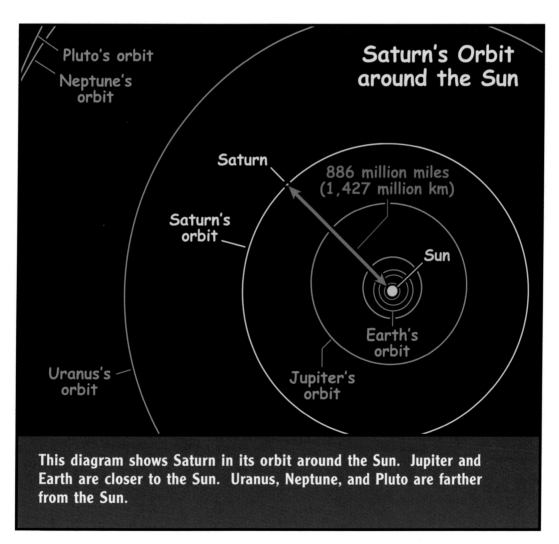

Pluto's orbit

Neptune's orbit

Saturn's Orbit around the Sun

Saturn

886 million miles (1,427 million km)

Saturn's orbit

Sun

Earth's orbit

Uranus's orbit

Jupiter's orbit

This diagram shows Saturn in its orbit around the Sun. Jupiter and Earth are closer to the Sun. Uranus, Neptune, and Pluto are farther from the Sun.

A year is the time a planet takes to travel once around the Sun. Saturn is more than nine times farther from the Sun than Earth is. That means Saturn's orbit is much longer than Earth's. A year on Saturn lasts 30 Earth years.

This artwork shows Saturn and other planets in orbit around the Sun. Saturn is the planet that's closest to us in this picture. The Sun shines brightly at the center.

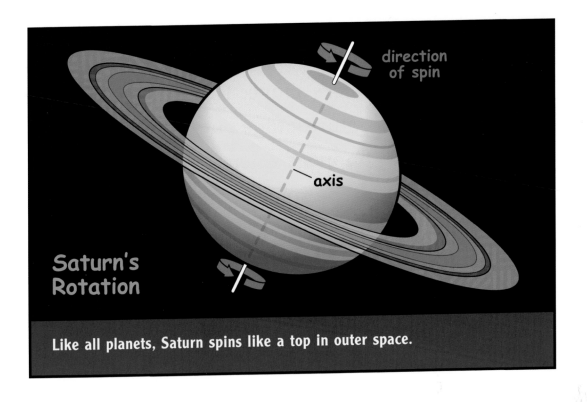

direction
of spin

axis

Saturn's
Rotation

Like all planets, Saturn spins like a top in outer space.

Planets also rotate (ROH-tayt). They spin around like a top. Each planet rotates on its axis. An axis is an imaginary line that goes through the center of the planet from top to bottom.

A day is the time a planet takes to rotate all the way around. Saturn rotates quickly. It takes about 10½ hours to rotate once. Earth takes 24 hours to rotate. So one day on Earth is more than twice as long as one day on Saturn.

Saturn's fast rotation does something strange to the planet's shape. The speedy spinning makes Saturn bulge out in the middle. The same thing happens when a person twirls around in a skirt. The spinning makes the skirt fly out into the air. Saturn's bulging middle makes it look like a squished ball.

Twirling makes this dancer's skirt fly away from her body. The same motion makes Saturn's center bulge.

In 1980, *Voyager I* flew by Saturn, taking pictures and sending them back to Earth. Who studied the pictures?

CHAPTER 3

SATURN UP CLOSE

No person has ever visited Saturn. But spacecraft have traveled there. Spacecraft travel from Earth to outer space. They take pictures and collect information.

Astronomers (uh-STRAH-nuh-muhrs) have studied this information. Astronomers are scientists who study outer space. They have learned a lot about Saturn.

Saturn's swirling gases look like giant bands across the planet.

Saturn is much bigger than Earth. But Saturn is not a solid planet like Earth. Saturn is mostly made up gases.

Gases are lighter than liquids and solids. If Earth and Saturn were the same size, Saturn would be much lighter than Earth. Saturn is even lighter than water. Imagine putting Saturn in a giant pool. The planet would float!

Each planet is made up of different layers. Saturn's outer layer is made of gases. This gas layer is called the atmosphere (AT-muhs-fir). Saturn's atmosphere is very thick.

Earth has an atmosphere too. Its atmosphere has oxygen in it. People breathe oxygen (OX-ih-jehn). Saturn's atmosphere has hydrogen and helium gases. So a person could not breathe the air on Saturn.

The atmosphere on Earth provides oxygen for us to breathe. Saturn's atmosphere has no oxygen.

Below Saturn's atmosphere are deep liquid layers. The liquid layers blend into the gas layers. So the planet has no real surface as Earth does.

Astronomers think that a solid ball of rock forms the center of the planet. This ball is tiny compared to the rest of the planet. But it is probably bigger than Earth.

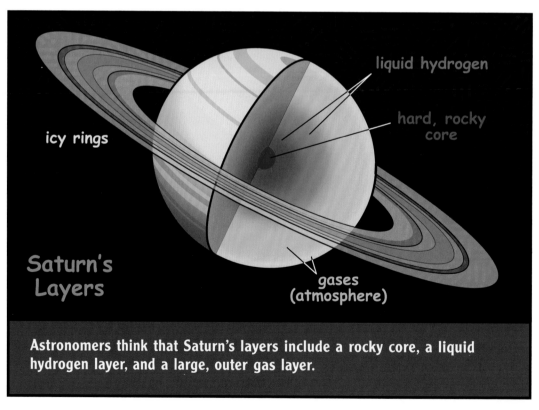

liquid hydrogen

hard, rocky core

icy rings

Saturn's Layers

gases (atmosphere)

Astronomers think that Saturn's layers include a rocky core, a liquid hydrogen layer, and a large, outer gas layer.

Ice freezes in the mustache and beard of a scientist in Antarctica. Saturn's outer layers are much colder than even Antarctica, the coldest place on Earth.

Saturn lies far from the Sun's warmth. So it is a cold place. Its outer temperature is about −288°F (−178°C). The coldest temperature ever recorded on Earth was −128°F (−89°C). Saturn's outer layers are much, much colder.

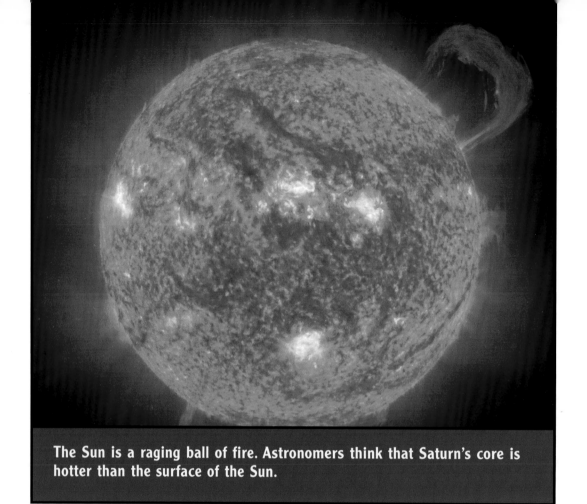

The Sun is a raging ball of fire. Astronomers think that Saturn's core is hotter than the surface of the Sun.

Under its atmosphere, Saturn is much warmer. Gravity pulls Saturn's liquid layers in toward the center. That force creates a lot of heat. Saturn may be as hot as 21,000°F (11,649°C) at its center. That's about twice as hot as the Sun's surface.

Saturn is the windiest planet in the solar system. Winds in its atmosphere move up to 1,100 miles (1,770 km) per hour. That's four times faster than winds in Earth's strongest tornadoes.

The winds push Saturn's clouds around its atmosphere. The clouds look like thick stripes going around the planet.

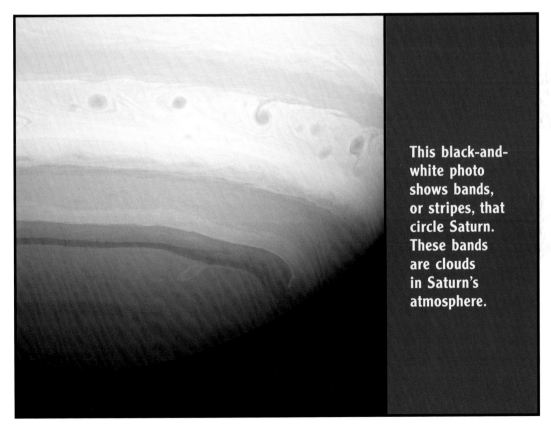

This black-and-white photo shows bands, or stripes, that circle Saturn. These bands are clouds in Saturn's atmosphere.

Saturn's atmosphere is a stormy place. The storms look like large spots on the planet. Many of these storms are thousands of miles wide. Some of them are even bigger than Earth.

Saturn's storms don't just last for hours or a few days. They can last weeks, months, or even years.

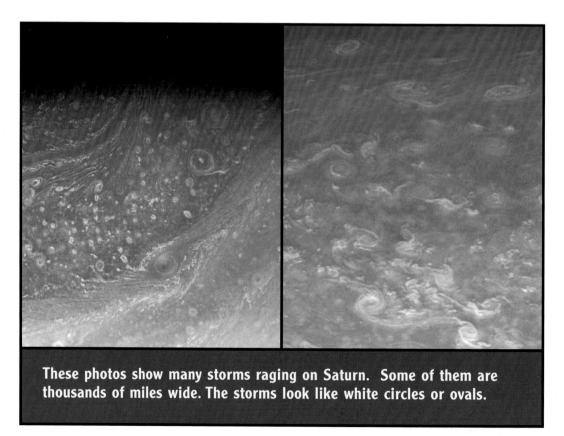

These photos show many storms raging on Saturn. Some of them are thousands of miles wide. The storms look like white circles or ovals.

This digital image makes Saturn (TOP) and Uranus appear to be of similar size. But Saturn is much bigger. Can you see the difference between Saturn's and Uranus's rings?

CHAPTER 4

RINGING THE PLANET

Saturn's nickname is the ringed giant. Jupiter, Uranus, and Neptune are also giant planets with rings. But Saturn's rings are the largest and brightest.

The *Cassini* spacecraft took this image of Saturn. That day, the Sun lit up each of the planet's rings.

Saturn's rings look like a Frisbee with a hole in the middle. But astronomers have discovered eight separate rings. Between some of the rings lie gaps of black space.

The rings are not solid circles. Each one is made of many chunks of ice and rock. The largest pieces are as big as a house. The smallest pieces are as tiny as a grain of sand. All of these pieces travel in an orbit around the planet. Together, they form Saturn's amazing rings.

An artist created this view of what Saturn's rings might look like. Chunks of ice, rock, and dust make up Saturn's rings.

Saturn's many moons are beyond its rings.
Saturn has at least 60 moons. Each moon
follows its own orbit around the planet.

ABOVE: The two bright spots in this photo are two of Saturn's moons. **LEFT:** Four moons can be seen in this photo. Below the rings are Dione (LEFT) and Titan (RIGHT). Prometheus is a bright dot touching the bottom of the rings. And the tiny speck high above the rings is Telesto.

TOP: Dione is an icy moon.
BOTTOM: Pandora is a moon that looks like a potato!

Saturn's largest moons are round like Earth's moon. Saturn's smaller moons look like giant rocks or potatoes. The moons are cold, icy places.

The giant moon Titan looms behind Saturn's rings. Titan is 3,200 miles (5,150 km) wide. The other moon in this photo, Epimetheus, is only 70 miles (113 km) wide.

One moon stands out from all the rest. Its name is Titan. Titan is the second-largest moon in the solar system. Titan is even larger than the planet Mercury.

Titan is the only moon with an atmosphere. Its atmosphere is ten times thicker than Earth's. The atmosphere makes Titan look bright orange.

Below the atmosphere are icy mountains and deep valleys. Titan also has rivers, lakes, and volcanoes. In some ways, it is like Earth was billions of years ago.

ABOVE: This photo shows a large island in the middle of a lake on Titan. The island is about the size of the island of Hawaii. RIGHT: Enceladus, another of Saturn's moons, is covered in ice.

Galileo Galilei used his telescope to view the night sky. What objects did he see?

CHAPTER 5
VISITING SATURN

People have wondered about Saturn for thousands of years. They knew it shone in the sky. But they didn't know how big it was. They didn't know about Saturn's rings or moons, either. Astronomers wanted to learn more about the planet.

Galileo Galilei was the first astronomer to see Saturn with a telescope. Galileo lived 400 years ago. Telescopes had just been invented. They did not work that well. Galileo's telescope gave him a blurry picture of Saturn. The rings looked like handles or ears. Galileo thought they might be moons.

a 3 volte maggiore

ma OOO, s

in questo autunno

Early telescopes still made faraway objects look fuzzy. Galileo made this drawing of Saturn in his notebook after seeing it through his telescope. His notebook was later made into a book.

About 50 years later, Christiaan Huygens discovered Saturn's rings. He had a stronger telescope than Galileo had. Huygens also discovered Titan, Saturn's largest moon.

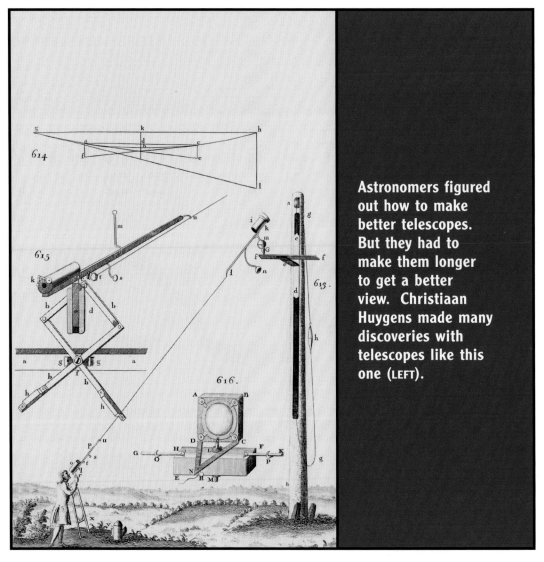

Astronomers figured out how to make better telescopes. But they had to make them longer to get a better view. Christiaan Huygens made many discoveries with telescopes like this one (LEFT).

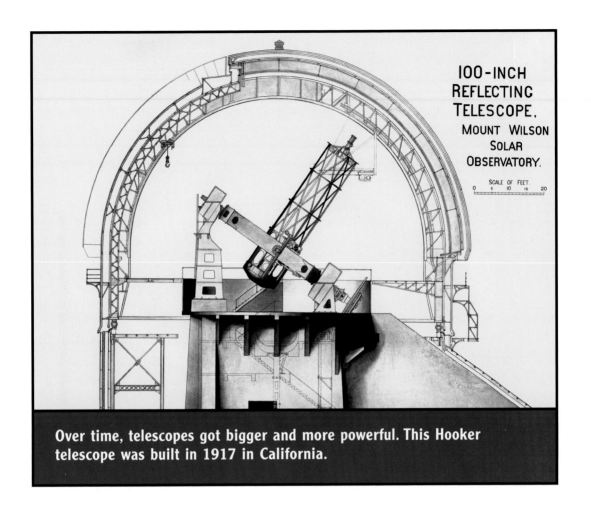

100-INCH
REFLECTING
TELESCOPE,
MOUNT WILSON
SOLAR
OBSERVATORY.

SCALE OF FEET.
0   5   10   15   20

Over time, telescopes got bigger and more powerful. This Hooker telescope was built in 1917 in California.

Through the years, scientists made better and better telescopes. Astronomers could see Saturn more and more clearly. They learned more about the planet. But spacecraft have taught astronomers the most about the ringed giant.

Pioneer 11 took this picture of Saturn in 1979.

The first spacecraft to visit Saturn was *Pioneer 11*. It was launched in 1973. It finally reached Saturn in 1979.

Voyager 1 and *Voyager 2* visited Saturn in the next two years. These two spacecraft took pictures of Saturn's atmosphere, rings, and moons.

Voyager 2 traveled to Saturn and sent this photo back to Earth.

A double spacecraft called *Cassini-Huygens* reached Saturn in 2004. At the planet, *Huygens* was dropped from *Cassini*. *Huygens* landed on Titan's surface. *Huygens* sent pictures and information back to Earth.

An artist made this image of *Huygens* on the surface of Titan.

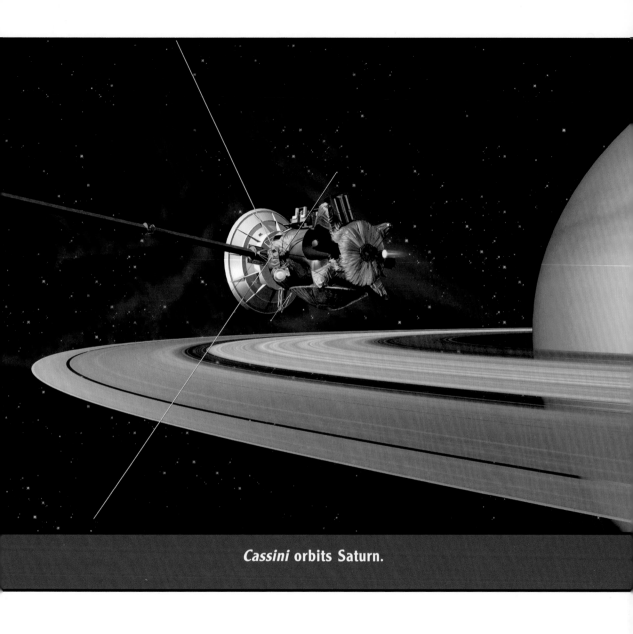

Cassini orbits Saturn.

Cassini orbited Saturn. Scientists learned more about Saturn from this mission. *Cassini* helped discover 42 of Saturn's 60 moons.

Cassini discovered that even one of Saturn's moons has rings!

Cassini also gave scientists a better understanding of Saturn's rings. It even even helped scientists discover rings around Saturn's moon Rhea.

Huygens took the first pictures of Titan's surface. These pictures allowed scientists to learn more about this mysterious moon.

Scientists plan to study information from *Cassini-Huygens* for years to come. They still have a lot to learn about Saturn.

Huygens took this picture of the surface of Titan. Titan's atmosphere makes the air look hazy and reddish.

ON SHARING A BOOK

When you share a book with a child, you show that reading is important. To get the most out of the experience, read in a comfortable, quiet place. Turn off the television and limit other distractions, such as telephone calls. Be prepared to start slowly. Take turns reading parts of this book. Stop occasionally and discuss what you're reading. Talk about the photographs. If the child begins to lose interest, stop reading. When you pick up the book again, revisit the parts you have already read.

BE A VOCABULARY DETECTIVE

The word list on page 5 contains words that are important in understanding the topic of this book. Be word detectives and search for the words as you read the book together. Talk about what the words mean and how they are used in the sentence. Do any of these words have more than one meaning? You will find the words defined in a glossary on page 46.

WHAT ABOUT QUESTIONS?

Use questions to make sure the child understands the information in this book. Here are some suggestions:

What does this picture show? What do you think we'll learn about next? Which planets are between Saturn and the Sun? What are Saturn's rings made of? What is the name of Saturn's biggest moon? Which gases make up Saturn? What is your favorite part of the book? Why?

If the child has questions, don't hesitate to respond with questions of your own, such as What do *you* think? Why? What is it that you don't know? If the child can't remember certain facts, turn to the index.

INTRODUCING THE INDEX

The index helps readers find information without searching through the whole book. Turn to the index on page 48. Choose an entry such as *spacecraft* and ask the child to use the index to find out how spacecraft help us learn about the planet. Repeat with as many entries as you like. Ask the child to point out the differences between an index and a glossary. (The index helps readers find information, while the glossary tells readers what words mean.)

SATURN

BOOKS

Hoffman, Sara. *The Little Book of Space*. Minnetonka, MN: Two-Can, 2005. In this book, the author describes the planets of the solar system as well as different missions to space.

Jeunesse, Gallimard, and Jean-Pierre Verdet. *The Universe*. New York: Scholastic Reference, 2007. Readers can explore the solar system as well as what lies beyond it.

Lauw, Darlene, and Lim Cheng Puay. *Earth and the Solar System*. New York: Crabtree, 2002. Lauw offers a hands-on understanding of our home planet and the solar system through activities and experiments.

Peddicord, Jane Ann. *Night Wonders*. Watertown, MA: Charlesbridge, 2005. Peddicord takes readers on an adventure to the planets and stars.

WEBSITES

Cassini-Huygens: Kid's Space
http://saturn.jpl.nasa.gov/kids/index.cfm
The official website of the Cassini-Huygens space mission is fact packed and includes fun activities for kids.

Extreme Space
http://solarsystem.nasa.gov/kids/index.cfm
The National Aeronautics and Space Administration (NASA) created this astronomy website just for kids.

Saturn
http://kids.nineplanets.org/saturn.htm
This astronomy website offers lots of information about the sixth planet in our solar system.

The Space Place
http://spaceplace.nasa.gov/en/kids/
Go to this Web page of NASA's for activities, quizzes, and games all about outer space.

GLOSSARY

asteroid (A-stur-oyd): a rocky body, much smaller than a planet, that exists in outer space.

asteroid belt: the group of asteroids in our solar system that orbit the Sun between Mars and Jupiter

astronomer (uh-STRAH-nuh-muhr): a scientist who studies outer space

atmosphere (AT-muhs-fir): the layer of gases that surrounds a planet

axis: an imaginary line that goes through a planet from top to bottom. A planet spins on its axis.

day: the time a planet takes to rotate once

elliptical (ih-LIHP-tih-cuhl): oval shaped

gas giant: a planet that is made up mostly of gases

Kuiper belt (KY-pur behlt): a region of outer space beyond Neptune that is filled with rocks, ice, and dwarf planets, including Pluto

orbit: the path of a planet, moon, or other object in space around the Sun or a planet. Orbit can also mean to move along this path.

rotate (ROH-tayt): to spin around like a top

solar system: a group of planets and other objects that travel around the Sun

spacecraft: machines that travel from Earth to outer space

telescope (TEH-luh-skohp): an instrument that makes faraway objects appear bigger and closer

year: the time a planet takes to orbit the Sun

INDEX

Pages listed in **bold** type refer to photographs.